READING POWER

In the Ring with Diamond Dallas Page

Michael Payan

The Rosen Publishing Group's

PowerKids Press ™
New York

1

To Al, Grace, and baby makes three...I love you guys!

Published in 2002 by The Rosen Publishing Group, Inc.
29 East 21st Street, New York, NY 10010

First Edition

Book Design: Michael Donnellan

Photo Credits: all photos by Colin Bowman.

Payan, Michael.
In the ring with Diamond Dallas Page / Michael Payan.
    p. cm. — (Wrestlers)
Includes bibliographical references (p.) and index.
  ISBN 0–8239–6048–X
1. Page, Diamond Dallas, 1949– —Juvenile literature. 2. Wrestlers—United States—Biography—Juvenile literature. [1. Page, Diamond Dallas, 1949–
2. Wrestlers.] I. Title.
  GV1196.D52 P39 2002
  796.812'092—dc21

                                                     2001000161

Manufactured in the United States of America

2

Contents

Diamond Dallas Page is a wrestler. Lots of people call him DDP for short.

When DDP wrestles, he likes to yell, "Bang!"

DDP grabs his opponent's head. His opponent is Saturn.

DDP lifts up a chair.

DDP flies through the air.

13

DDP holds Goldberg's
arm. He squeezes it tight.

DDP wrestles Ric Flair outside of the ring.

DDP throws Hollywood Hulk Hogan across the ring.

19

DDP lifts his belt above his head in victory. DDP wins again!

Glossary

opponent (uh-POH-nent) A person who is on the opposite side in a game or match.

ring (RING) A square-shaped, enclosed area where wrestling matches take place.

victory (VIK-tor-ee) To have success over your opponent, to win.

Here is another book to read about Diamond Dallas Page:

Diamond Dallas Page: The Story of the Wrestler They Call 'Diamond Dallas Page' (Pro Wrestling Legends)
by Jacqueline Mudge.
Chelsea House Publishers
(October 2000)

To learn more about Diamond Dallas Page, check out these Web sites:

www.ddpbang.com
www.wcw.com/2000/superstars/ddp

Index

Word Count: *77*

Note to Librarians, Teachers, and Parents

If reading is a challenge, Reading Power is a solution! Reading Power is perfect for readers who want high-interest subject matter at an accessible reading level. These fact-filled, photo-illustrated books are designed for readers who want straightforward vocabulary, engaging topics, and a manageable reading experience. With clear picture/text correspondence, leveled Reading Power books put the reader in charge. Now readers have the power to get the information they want and the skills they need in a user-friendly format.